This page contains important information about using this Pet Recipe Collection safely and responsibly. Please take a moment to read it before you dive in.

Disclaimer

This Pet Recipe Collection contains general information only and is not a substitute for professional veterinary care. Always consult a qualified veterinarian before making decisions about your pet's health, diet, or treatment.

Product & Service Disclaimer

Any mention of products, services, brands, or websites in this Pet Recipe Collection is for informational purposes only. We do not provide any guarantee or warranty as to their safety, quality, effectiveness, availability, or suitability for your individual pet.

You are solely responsible for any decisions regarding the use of such products or services. The publishers of **Pawfect Treats** accept no responsibility and shall not be held liable for any loss, injury, claim, damage, or expense arising from reliance on, or use of, such information.

Copyright Notice

No part of this Pet Recipe Collection may be reproduced, distributed, transmitted, or sold in any form or by any means, including photocopying, printing, recording, or electronic or mechanical methods, without prior written permission from the publisher. This Pet Recipe Collection is provided for personal use only. Commercial use, resale, or distribution is strictly prohibited.

Publisher Contact Details

The Ultimate Bill Survival Guides
Website: billsurvivalguides.com
Email: contact@billsurvivalguides.com
Follow us: Facebook | X | Instagram | TikTok | YouTube

Pawfect Treats

20 quick & easy treat recipes for dogs & cats

Fun treat recipes for wagging tails and happy whiskers.

Welcome to **Pawfect Treats**, your free homemade recipe collection filled with simple, healthy, and fun ideas to spoil your pets.

Inside you'll find **20 quick and easy homemade recipes**, with **10 for dogs** and **10 for cats**, all made using everyday ingredients you can trust. From crunchy biscuits to no-bake bites and refreshing frozen snacks, there's something here for every wagging tail and curious whisker.

Making your own pet treats is not only fun, it's also a great way to show your furry companions just how much you love them. You'll know exactly what's going into every bite, and you might even save a little on store-bought snacks along the way.

Every recipe is designed to be quick to prepare, easy to follow, and most importantly, pet-approved. Just remember to consider your pet's unique dietary needs and chat with your vet if you're unsure about introducing new foods.

So roll up your sleeves, grab a mixing bowl, and let's create some tasty memories together.

peanut butter oatie bites

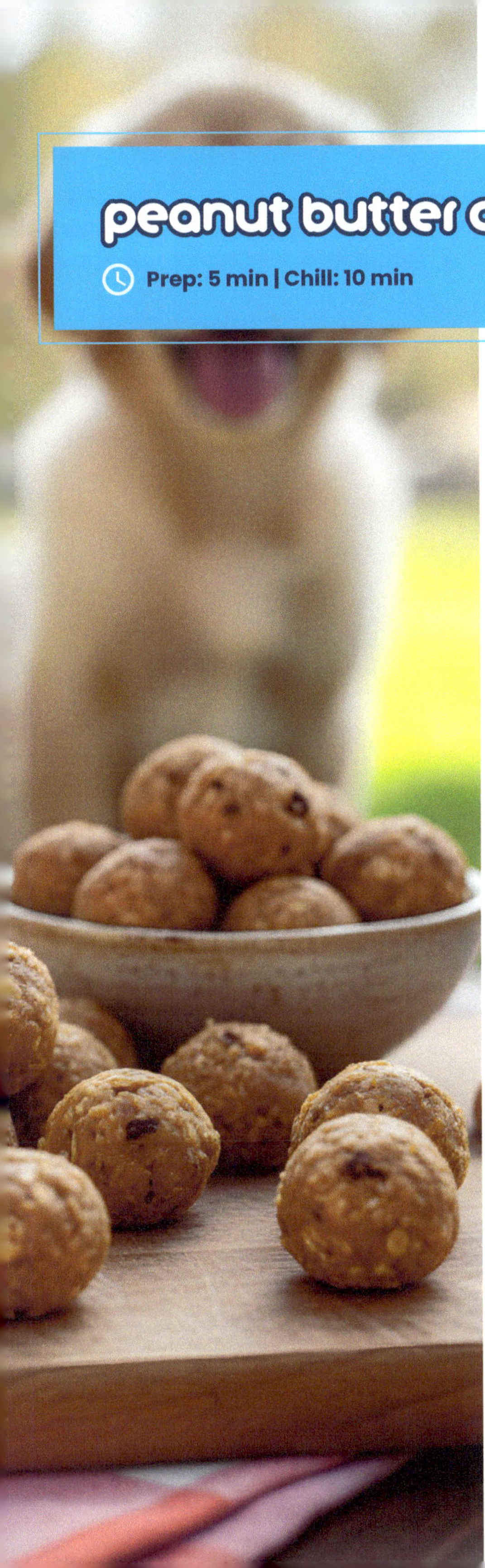

Peanut Butter Oatie Bites are chewy, nutty, and bite-sized. These no-bake snacks are made with oats, peanut butter, and honey. Perfect for training sessions or just spoiling your pooch with something wholesome.

ingredients

- 1 cup rolled oats
- ½ cup creamy peanut butter (xylitol-free)
- ¼ cup honey

directions

1 In a mixing bowl, combine the rolled oats, peanut butter, and honey.

2 Mix until well combined.

3 Roll the mixture into small balls, about the size of a marble.

4 Place the balls on a plate or baking sheet and refrigerate for 10 minutes to firm up.

5 Serve the treats to your furry friend.

NOTE: Use Peanut Butter that is xylitol-free. Xylitol is toxic to dogs.

frozen yogurt nibbles

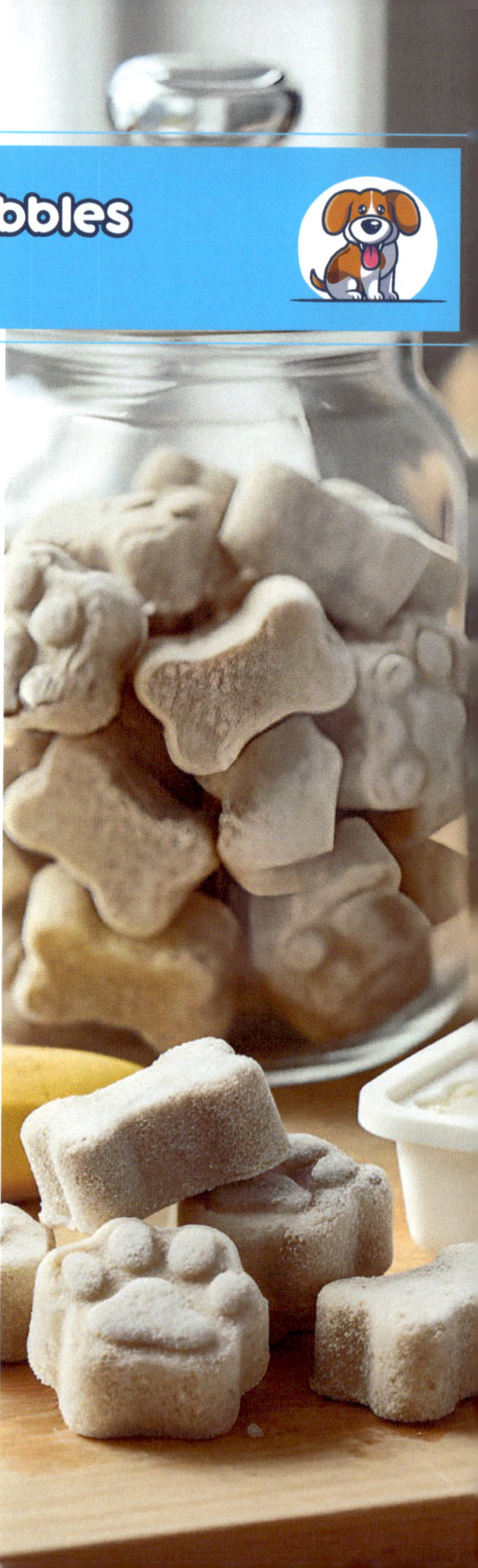

Cool and creamy, these **Frozen Yogurt Nibbles** are a refreshing treat for hot days. With banana and peanut butter blended in, they're simple, healthy, and always a hit with dogs.

ingredients

- 1 cup plain Greek yogurt
- 1 ripe banana
- ¼ cup creamy peanut butter (xylitol-free)

directions

1. In a blender or food processor, combine the yogurt, banana, and peanut butter.

2. Blend until smooth.

3. Pour the mixture into an ice cube tray and freeze for at least 2 hours or until firm.

4. Pop the treats out of the ice cube tray and store in a freezer-safe container.

5. Serve the treats to your furry friend.

apple crunch pupcakes

🕐 **Prep: 10 min | Bake: 10–12 min**

ingredients

- ½ cup unsweetened applesauce
- ¼ cup honey
- 1 egg
- 1 cup whole wheat flour
- 1 tsp baking powder
- ½ tsp cinnamon
- ½ cup grated apple

directions

1 Preheat the oven to 350°F (175°C) and line a muffin tin with paper liners.

2 In a mixing bowl, whisk together the applesauce, honey, and egg.

3 Add the flour, baking powder, and cinnamon to the bowl and mix until well combined.

4 Fold in the grated apple.

5 Spoon the batter into the muffin cups, filling each about ⅔ full.

6 Bake for 10-12 minutes or until a toothpick inserted comes out clean.

7 Let the Pupcakes cool completely before serving.

chicken & rice bites

🕐 **Prep: 8 min | Chill: 10 min**

Simple and satisfying, these wholesome **Chicken & Rice Bites** combine chicken, rice, and parsley for a tasty, protein-rich treat. Easy to prepare and perfect for quick rewards.

ingredients

- 1 cup cooked and shredded chicken
- 1 cup cooked white rice
- ¼ cup chopped fresh parsley

directions

1 In a mixing bowl, combine the shredded chicken, cooked rice, and chopped parsley.

2 Roll the mixture into small balls, about the size of a marble.

3 Place the balls on a plate or baking sheet and refrigerate for 10 minutes to firm up.

4 Give your pet a tasty reward.

PAWFECT TREATS © 2025

sweet potato chewies

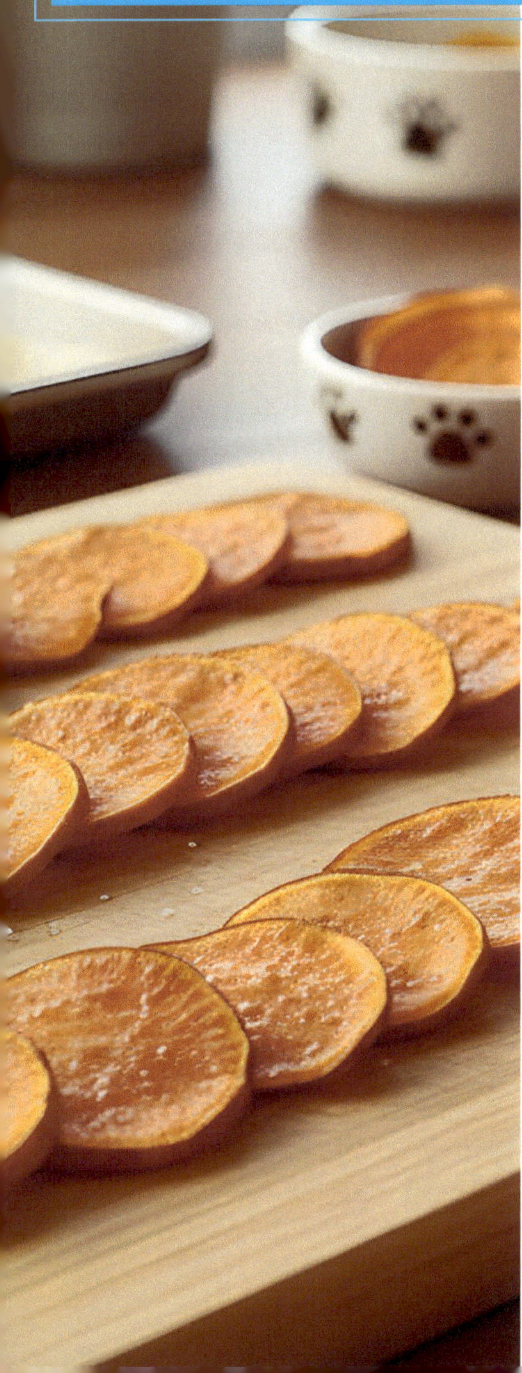

Naturally sweet and chewy, these **Sweet Potato Chewies** are one-ingredient treats that are as healthy as they are tasty. Packed with fiber and vitamins, they're a guilt-free snack your dog will love.

ingredients

- 1 sweet potato

directions

1 Preheat the oven to 250°F (120°C) and line a baking sheet with parchment paper.

2 Slice the sweet potato into thin rounds, about ⅛ inch thick.

3 Place the rounds on the prepared baking sheet.

4 Bake for 2-3 hours or until the rounds are dried out and chewy.

5 Let the chews cool completely before giving your pooch a tasty reward.

pumpkin & peanut butter drops

🕐 **Prep: 10 min | Chill: 30 min**

Soft, chewy, and full of flavor, these no-bake **Pumpkin & Peanut Butter Drops** are quick to make and perfect for rewarding good behavior.

ingredients

- 1 cup canned pumpkin puree
- ½ cup peanut butter (xylitol-free)
- ¼ cup coconut flour

directions

1 In a mixing bowl, combine the pumpkin puree and peanut butter.

2 Add the coconut flour and mix until well combined.

3 Drop spoonfuls of the mixture onto a plate or baking sheet lined with parchment paper.

4 Refrigerate the drops for at least 30 minutes or until firm.

5 Serve the drops to your pup as a treat.

  PAWFECT TREATS © 2025

cheesy apple bites

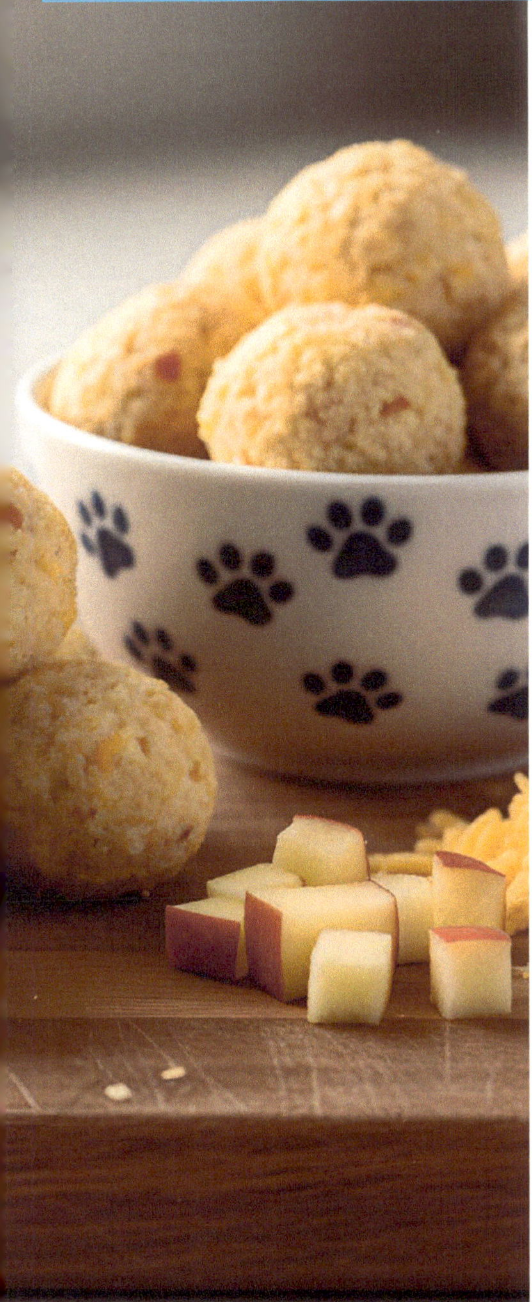

These delightful **Cheesy Apple Bites** are a simple and flavorful no-bake treat your dog will adore. Combining the savory goodness of grated cheddar cheese with the sweet crunch of finely chopped apple and a touch of coconut flour, these small, wholesome balls are easy to prepare for a delicious and healthy snack!

ingredients

- 1 cup grated cheddar cheese
- ½ cup finely chopped apple
- ¼ cup coconut flour

directions

1 In a mixing bowl, combine the grated cheese, chopped apple, and coconut flour.

2 Mix until well combined.

3 Roll the mixture into small balls and place on a plate or baking sheet.

4 Refrigerate for at least 30 minutes before serving.

blueberry oat bites

🕒 **Prep: 8 min | Chill: 30 min**

Bursting with natural sweetness, these **Blueberry Oat Bites** are a healthy, fruity snack. Simple to prepare and perfect for dogs who love a fresh flavor.

ingredients

- 1 cup rolled oats
- ½ cup fresh blueberries
- ¼ cup unsweetened applesauce
- ¼ cup honey

directions

1. In a mixing bowl, combine the rolled oats, blueberries, applesauce, and honey.

2. Mix until well combined.

3. Drop spoonfuls of the mixture onto a plate or baking sheet.

4. Refrigerate for at least 30 minutes before serving to your dog.

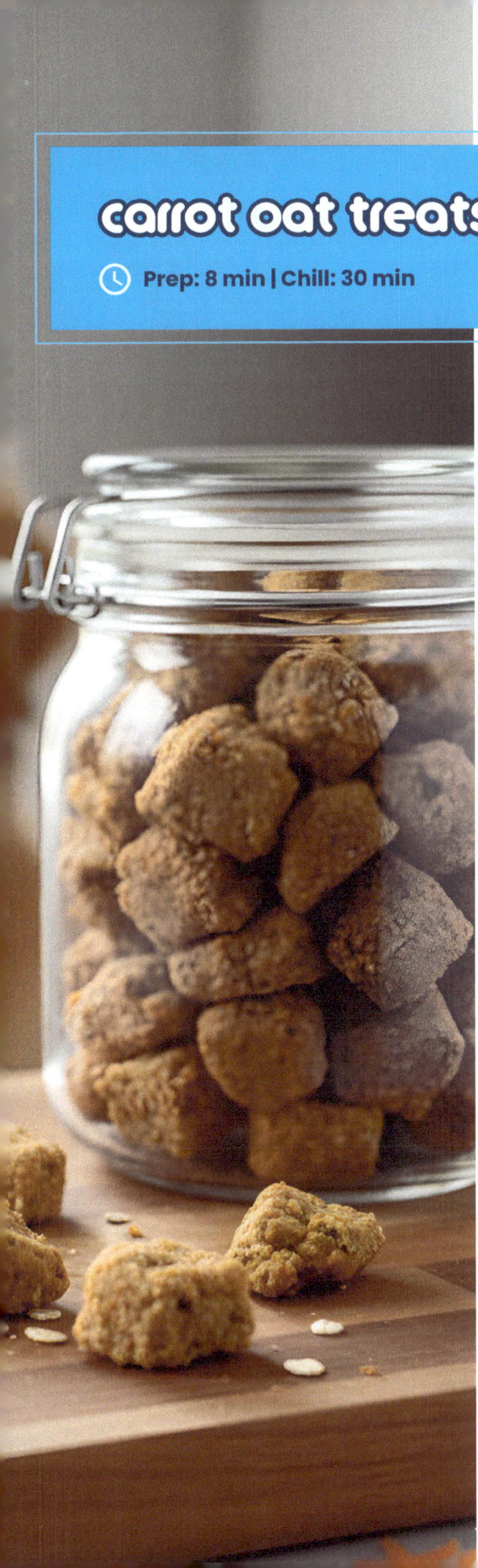

carrot oat treats

Nutritious and naturally sweet, these no-bake **Carrot Oat Treats** combine oats, applesauce, and honey into a tasty, wholesome snack your dog will happily crunch on.

These easy-to-prepare bites are packed with flavor and healthy ingredients.

ingredients

- 1 cup rolled oats
- ½ cup shredded carrots
- ¼ cup unsweetened applesauce
- ¼ cup honey

directions

1 In a mixing bowl, combine the rolled oats, shredded carrots, applesauce, and honey.

2 Mix until well combined.

3 Roll the mixture into small balls and place on a plate or baking sheet.

4 Refrigerate for at least 30 minutes before serving.

sweet potato pb bites

🕐 **Prep: 10 min | Chill: 30 min**

Creamy peanut butter and mashed sweet potato make these soft, no-bake **Sweet Potato PB Bites** a favorite. They're quick to prepare, nutritious, and a delicious way to treat your furry friend.

ingredients

- ½ cup mashed sweet potato
- ¼ cup peanut butter (xylitol-free)
- ¼ cup coconut flour

directions

1 In a mixing bowl, combine the mashed sweet potato and peanut butter.

2 Add the coconut flour and mix until well combined.

3 Roll the mixture into small balls and place on a plate or baking sheet.

4 Refrigerate for at least 30 minutes before serving to your pup.

tuna catnip crunchies

Prep: 10 min | Bake: 10 min

Savory and satisfying, these Tuna Catnip Crunchies bake up with a light crunch.

They're simple to prepare and packed with flavors that cats can't resist.

ingredients

- 5 oz (150g) canned tuna
- 1 cup brown rice flour
- 1 tbsp flaxmeal, mixed with 3 tbsp water; let sit in the fridge for 15 min
- 1 tbsp olive oil
- 1 tbsp catnip

directions

1 Blend tuna, flax mixture, flour, and oil until smooth, then stir in catnip.

2 Roll into small balls and place on a lined tray.

3 Flatten with a spoon, bake at 350°F (175°C) for 10 minutes.

4 Cool and store in the fridge for up to 7 days.

chicken heart bites

🕐 **Prep: 10 min | Bake: 10 min**

Wholesome and protein-rich, these **Chicken Heart Bites** are shaped into fun little snacks. They're an easy, homemade way to show your cat extra love.

ingredients

- 5 oz (150g) cooked chicken
- 1 cup oat flour
- 1 tbsp flaxmeal, mixed with 3 tbsp water; let sit in the fridge for 15 min
- 1 tbsp olive oil
- 1 tbsp catnip

directions

1 Blend cooked chicken, oat flour, flax mixture, olive oil, and catnip into a smooth dough.

2 Roll dough flat (¼ inch thick) on baking paper.

3 Cut into shapes with cookie cutters.

4 Bake at 350ºF (175ºC) for 10 minutes, then store in the fridge for up to 7 days.

salmon sweet potato snacks

Nutritious and colourful, these **Salmon Sweet Potato Snacks** are freezer-friendly and fun to make.

Packed with antioxidants, they're a tasty snack for curious cats.

ingredients

- 14 oz (400g) salmon
- 1 ½ cups sweet potato, baked and mashed
- 1 ½ cups rolled oats
- Silicone mold for the freezer

directions

1. Cut salmon into small pieces.

2. Mix salmon with sweet potato in a bowl.

3. Pulse oats and parsley, then stir into the mixture.

4. Spoon into molds and freeze for a few hours.

catnip super tonic

🕐 **Prep: 3 min**

Catnip Super Tonic is a quick, refreshing drink made with chicken stock and catnip.

It's an easy way to keep your kitty hydrated while giving them something extra special. Fast to prepare and perfect for a quick kitty pick-me-up.

ingredients

- 1 cup warm water
- ¼ tsp chicken bouillon powder (no onion/garlic - low sodium)
- 3 tbsp catnip

directions

1 Pour 1 cup of warm water into a jar or container.

2 Add the chicken stock powder and catnip to the water.

3 Secure the lid and shake well until the stock is fully dissolved.

4 Pour the tonic into your cat's bowl and serve right away.

     PAWFECT TREATS © 2025

crunchy cat croutons

🕐 **Prep: 10 min | Bake: 12–15 min**

Golden and bite-sized, these baked **Crunchy Cat Croutons** are made with tuna and a hint of catnip. They're crunchy, flavorful, and simple to prepare. A fantastic, healthy reward for your feline friend.

ingredients

- 15 oz (425g) can of tuna, drained
- 1 tbsp dried catnip
- 1-2 tbsp water
- 1 cup coconut flour
- 1 egg
- 1 tbsp extra-light olive oil

directions

1 Preheat oven to 350°F (180°C).

2 Blend all ingredients in a food processor.

3 Shape into small croutons, place on a lined baking sheet, and bake for 12–15 minutes until browned.

4 Cool completely, then store in the fridge in an airtight container for up to 7 days.

catnip beef crumble

🕐 **Prep: 10 min | Bake: 8 min | Cool: 10 min**

Savoury and simple, this **Catnip Beef Crumble** mixes beef and catnip for a flavor cats adore.

It bakes quickly into a protein-rich treat with a satisfying crunch that your cat will love.

ingredients

- 1 lb (450g) ground beef
- 2 eggs, beaten
- 2 tbsp catnip
- Aluminum Foil
- Large mixing bowl

directions

1 Combine all ingredients in a large bowl.

2 Spread mixture evenly on a foil-lined baking sheet.

3 Bake at low to medium heat for 8 minutes (drain excess fat if needed).

4 Let dry and cool before serving.

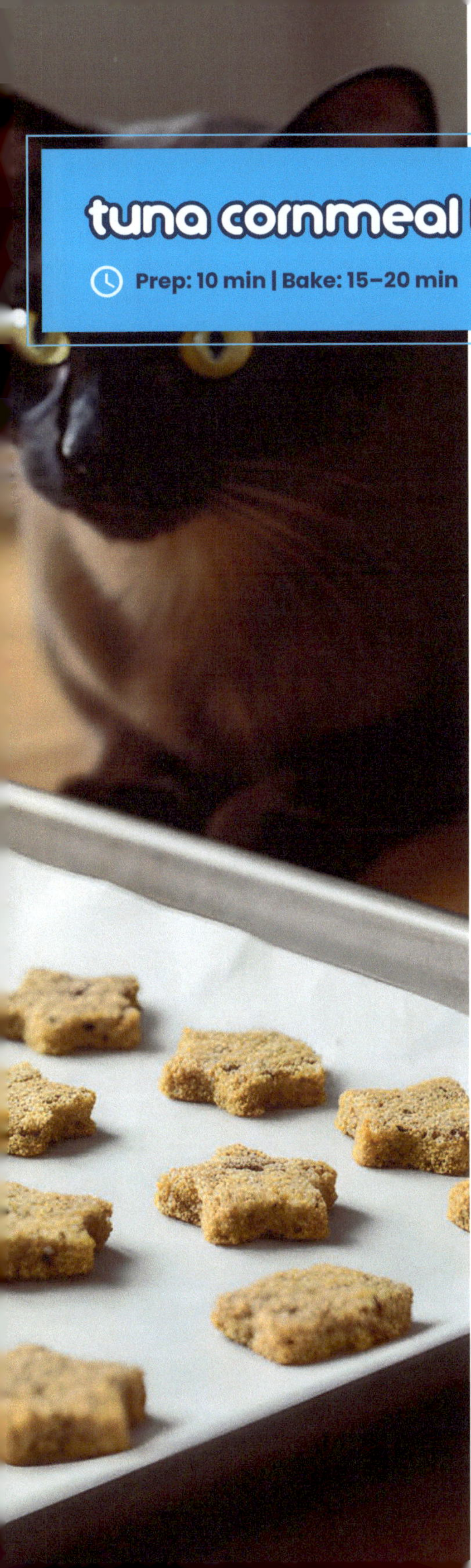

tuna cornmeal bakes

Crunchy and hearty, these **Tuna Cornmeal Bakes** are oven-baked into small, flavorful bites.

They're easy to prepare and bake into a savory, satisfying snack your feline friend will love.

ingredients

- 6 oz (170g) undrained tuna
- 1 cup flour
- 1 cup cornmeal
- 1 egg
- 2 tbsp water
- Cookie/biscuit cutter
- Lined Baking paper

directions

1 Preheat oven to 340°F (170°C).

2 Mix all ingredients in a bowl until soft dough forms.

3 Rest dough for 10 minutes.

4 Roll out on cornmeal, cut into shapes.

5 Bake 15–20 minutes, cool before serving.

Cheesy, savory, and ready in minutes, these no-bake **Tuna Cheese Balls** are quick to prepare and packed with protein. A wholesome, delicious reward your cat will enjoy.

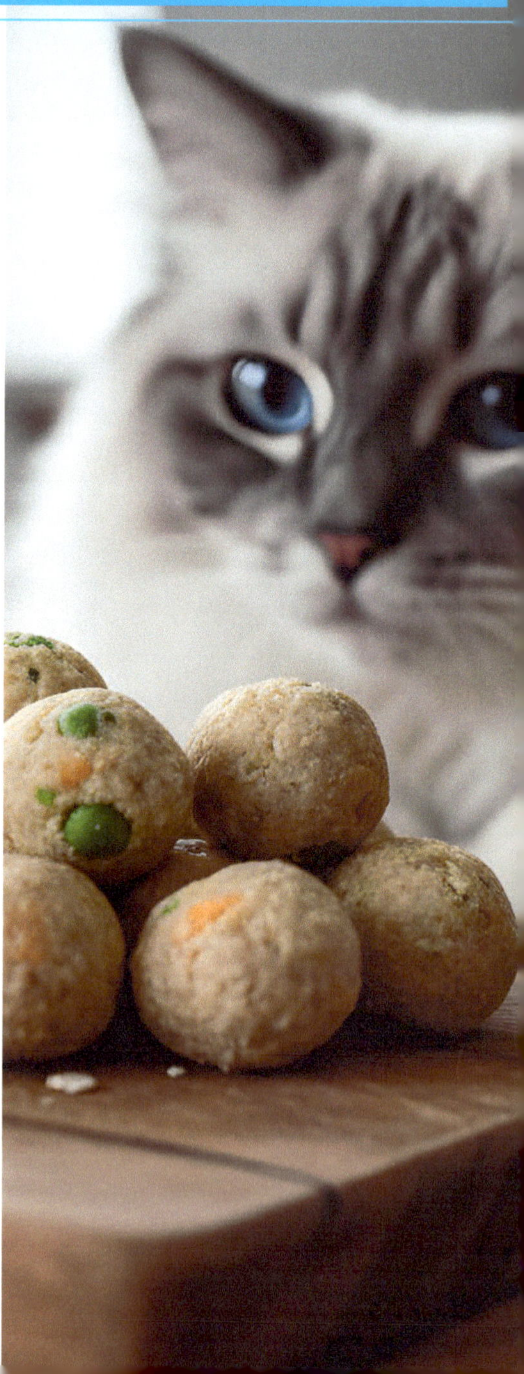

ingredients

- 1 tbsp grated Parmesan cheese
- ½ cup canned tuna
- ⅓ cup peas (frozen or canned)
- ¼ cup oats
- Vegetable oil

directions

1. Put the tuna, cheese, peas, and oats in a blender and mix. Gradually add vegetable oil until a dough forms.

2. Scoop out tablespoons of mixture and roll into balls.

3. Store in an airtight container in the fridge for up to 10 days.

chicken sardine mash

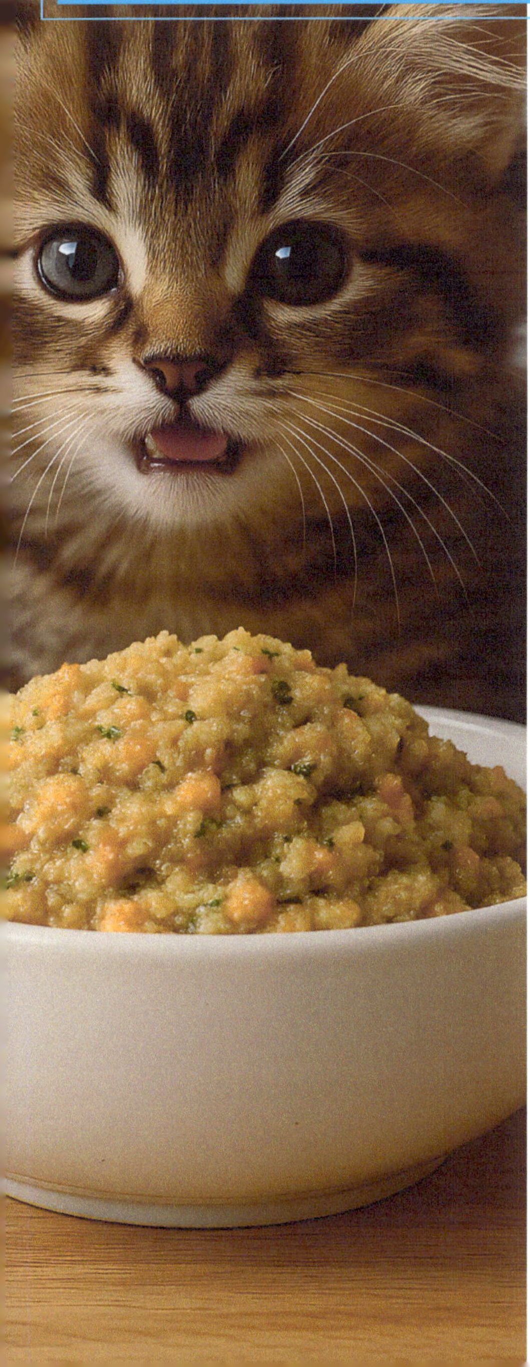

Rich in protein and nutrients, this **Chicken Sardine Mash** blends chicken and sardines with roasted veggies and herbs for a hearty, wholesome treat that's easy to prepare.

ingredients

- 2 lb (1 kg) boneless, skinless chicken
- 1 carrot
- 1 potato
- 1 butternut squash
- 1 can of whole sardines
- 3 tsp olive oil, plus extra
- 2 tsp fresh herbs (such as oregano, sage or thyme)

directions

1 Peel and chop veggies, toss with olive oil.

2 Bake at 375ºF (190ºC) 30 minutes.

3 Mash baked veggies with a fork.

4 Sauté chicken pieces, add sardines to heat through.

5 Combine everything with herbs, then serve in small portions.

carrot catnip crunchies

🕐 **Prep: 10 min | Bake: 12 min**

Crunchy and colorful, these **Carrot Catnip Crunchies** are baked squares of flavorful fun. Packed with natural goodness, they're a healthy and wholesome way to treat your kitty!

ingredients

- 2 tbsp oil (coconut or olive oil)
- 1 ¼ cups flour (all-purpose or oat)
- 1 tbsp dried catnip (optional)
- ¾ cup finely shredded carrot
- 1 large egg, lightly beaten
- Cold water as needed

directions

1 Preheat oven to 375°F (190°C), line tray.

2 Mix oil, flour, catnip, carrots, and egg into dough.

3 Roll to ¼ inch on floured surface.

4 Prick, cut into ½ inch squares, place on baking tray.

5 Bake 12 min, cool, and store airtight.

loved these recipes?

We hope you've enjoyed this **collection of 20 homemade pet treat recipes** to spoil your furry friends.

Now take the next step: discover how to keep treat time safe and protect your pets from hidden everyday food dangers.

Pet Safety: Toxic Foods & Hazards Quick Reference Guide

✔ Complete list of toxic foods, medications, plants & everyday hazards

✔ Clear panels + photos for fast answers

✔ Printable fridge chart for emergencies

✔ Vet-approved info for pet owners

Normally **$10**, but grab your copy today for just **$7**

👉 Scan the **QR Code** or visit **billsurvivalguides.com** and get your copy today

Keep your pets safe, happy, and healthy every day

PAWFECT TREATS © 2025

cut vet bills

Unlock simple, proven ways to **spend less at the vet** without cutting care, with checklists and insider tips you can use today.

Learn how to shop smarter for meds, avoid pricey mistakes, and plan for emergencies while **protecting your bank balance**.

The Ultimate Vet Bills Survival Guide

- 54 pages of practical strategies to save on dog and cat vet costs
- Insider tips and step-by-step checklists to start saving now
- Bonus resources pack (7 tools & guides, $90 value) included free
- Free lifetime updates, so your guide always stays current

Normally **$27**, but grab your copy today for just **$17**

👉 Scan the **QR Code** or visit **billsurvivalguides.com** and get your copy today

Care for your pet, without the financial stress

PAWFECT TREATS © 2025